Let's Talk A[bout]

FEELING FRUSTRATED

A PERSONAL FEELINGS BOOK

Written by Joy Berry   **Illustrated by Roey**

GOLD STAR PUBLISHING ™

Hello, my name is George.
I'd like to tell you a story
about my friend, Sam.

This is Sam.
Sometimes Sam
feels frustrated.

Sometimes Sam is not able
to do what he wants to do.
Sam feels frustrated.

4

Sometimes things do not work
the way they are supposed
to work.
Sam feels frustrated.

7

Sometimes situations do not
work out the way Sam
wants them to.
Sam feels frustrated.

When you feel frustrated,
you feel disappointed
and discouraged.

11

When you are frustrated,
you might want to

- cry,
- scream,
- yell, or
- jump up and down.

It is OK for you to do these things as long as you do not disturb other people while you are doing them.

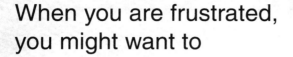

When you are frustrated, you might
want to hit or kick things.
It is OK to do this as long as your
hitting or kicking does not
hurt anyone or damage anything.
It is also OK for you to do this
as long as you do not
hurt yourself.

Try not to become frustrated when you are not able to do what you want to do. Sometimes it is helpful for you to slow down.

- Stop what you are doing.
- Count to ten.
- Start again and work more slowly.

17

Sometimes slowing down
might not improve the
situation. If it does not,
ask someone to help you.

19

If you still feel frustrated after someone has helped you, here are some things you can do:

- Stop what you are doing.
- Try again another time.

21

Try not to become frustrated when you cannot get something to work the way it is supposed to work. Instead, check to see if you are using the item correctly.

23

Try not to become frustrated
when something is not working
the way it is supposed to work.
Instead, find out what is wrong
with the item and what
can be done to get it
to work properly.

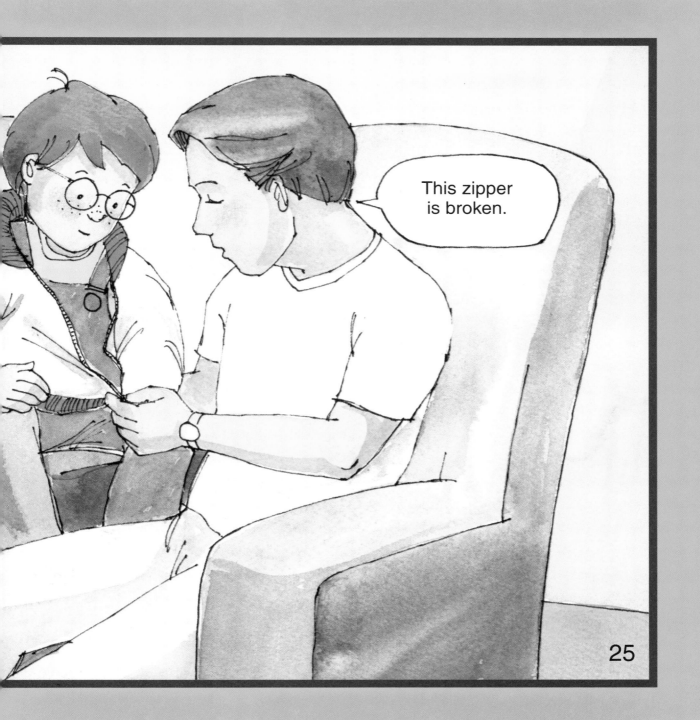

Do not continue to do
things that make you
feel frustrated.

Try not to get frustrated when
situations do not work out
the way you want them to.
It helps when you remember
that you cannot have your
way all of the time.

29

Try to make the best out of situations that do not go the way you planned.

- Maintain a positive attitude.
- Do whatever you can do to make every situation a positive one.

Remember that everyone feels frustrated at one time or another, so do not feel ashamed about feeling frustrated. Instead, do things that will make you feel better whenever you are frustrated.

What do you do when you feel frustrated?